A High School Curriculum
for Leadership

A HIGH SCHOOL CURRICULUM FOR LEADERSHIP

For the Academically Gifted in Catholic High Schools

Americo D. Lapati, Ph.D.

BOOKMAN ASSOCIATES :: New York

NIHIL OBSTAT

Rev. Robert C. Newbold, Ph.D.
Census Librorum

IMPRIMATUR

Russell J. McVinney, D.D., LL.D.
Bishop of Providence
Providence, R. I., May 6, 1961

MANUFACTURED IN THE UNITED STATES OF AMERICA BY
UNITED PRINTING SERVICES, INC.
NEW HAVEN, CONN.

TO MY TEACHERS
IN GRATITUDE FOR
EXAMPLES OF
INSPIRING LEADERSHIP

Contents

Tables

Introduction

Much discussion is carried on today relative to the merits and demerits of American education. Foreign systems of education have been singled out as being superior. Softness, an inevitable by-product of materialistic living, has been said to characterize our system of education. In the limelight of this criticism by both lay and educational leaders has been the high-school curriculum.

This volume traces, first, the historical development of the American high school; for the present evaluation of the high school should be seen in the historical context in which it has developed. We are all children of the past to some degree, and the present criticism of the American high school should be interpreted in the light of the role that this particular educational institution has played in American life. Such an historical analysis can lead to the distinctions that should be made for an adequate appraisal of the American high school.

Having considered the role of the high school in democratic America, together with its present criticism, we attempt to offer a philosophy for a curriculum for leadership. Such a curriculum should be regarded as a necessity in a democracy; for trained leaders as well as an educated citizenry are indispensable to the preservation of the ideals of freedom. Accordingly, the philosophy of a curriculum for leadership is discussed, with the necessary practical details required for putting this philosophy to work in a curriculum.

A *High School Curriculum for Leadership*

With the philosophy of the curriculum established, the placing of subjects in an over-all pattern is attempted. In the plethora of suggestions offered to "tighten up" the curriculum in our high schools the chief method of curriculum improvement and revision that has been adopted is the one by addition and subtraction. The mere taking out, or adding into, of a particular subject or group of subjects in the curriculum does not fulfill the principles underlying the development of a meaningful curriculum. Unless subjects are arranged to fit into a united whole, a meaningful pattern, the student's mind cannot perceive the desired broad horizons of knowledge. Some subject matter may have to be sacrificed to achieve this objective. Yet the study of isolated facts should always be kept inferior to the study of the broad outlines of knowledge, into which the facts can be better fitted later.

A curriculum for leadership cannot by its very nature be a curriculum for all. It is aimed at an intellectual elite. Admiral Hyman G. Rickover, a critic of American education and an advocate of the power of free and independent thinking, has called for the development to the fullest potential of the creative minds in our democracy.[1] Recognition given to talent does not make the ideas of democracy and equality contradictory. Diversity of talent postulates diversity of training. More common is the opinion of the American people becoming that

> the future of our country and of democracy as a way of life depends to a considerable degree upon the widespread recognition and development of our greatest resource—gifted children and youth.[2]

Introduction

As this curriculum for leadership is suggested primarily for Catholic high schools, mention ought to be made of the recent appraisals of Catholic intellectual life in the United States. A need has always existed for Catholic intellectual leadership. Pope Pius XI, in his encyclical on "The Christian Priesthood," urged members of the clergy to be interested not only in the ecclesiastical sciences but in all branches of knowledge;[3] for their philosophical and theological training forms a strong foundation and center upon which and from which all knowledge should stem and receive its inspiration. Yet the clergy and religious alone cannot possibly provide the scholars required for intellectual leadership in every field. The laity is urgently needed. Lay leaders in intellectual endeavors and research fulfill the call to Catholic action. Speaking at the Third Plenary Council of Baltimore, Bishop John Lancaster Spalding brought out the value that intellectual leadership has for American Catholicism.

> When our zeal for intellectual excellence shall have raised up men who will take place among the first writers and thinkers of their day their very presence will become the most persuasive of arguments to teach the world that no best gift is at war with the spirit of Catholic faith.[4]

Despite the challenging opportunity that Bishop Spalding offered Americans some seventy-five years ago, the present appraisal of American Catholic intellectual leadership has been that

> the weakest aspect of the Church in this country lies in its failure to produce national leaders and to exercise commanding influence in intellectual circles.[5]

A *High School Curriculum for Leadership*

Although there are a number of reasons that account for a lack of leadership of American Catholics in intellectual affairs, the situation cannot be accepted in smug complacency. This work accepts the challenge for us to rise from our intellectual stupor by proposing a high-school curriculum for leadership.

Future leaders must be singled out. By the use of intelligence and achievement tests, from the observation and judgment of teachers, and as a result of the expressed determination on the part of students desirous of pursuing a challenging intellectual training, a select group in every large Catholic high school can undertake the suggested curriculum for leadership. Both Church and country need intellectual leadership. We should then aim, in the words of Bishop John J. Wright, for an "Apostolate of distinction."[6]

A High School Curriculum
for Leadership

CHAPTER ONE

The High School in Democratic America

AN educated citizenry has always been considered essential for American democracy. The founding fathers of our country gave little hope to the success of the American political experiment if ignorance characterized the people. George Washington's *Farewell Address* advised:

> Promote then as an object of primary importance, Institutions for the general diffusion of knowledge. In proportion as the structure of government gives force to public opinion, it is essential that public opinion should be enlightened.

Daniel Webster forcefully declared that "on the diffusion of education among the people rests the preservation and perpetuation of our free institutions."[1] The words of John Madison are also provocative:

> A popular Government, without popular information, or the means of acquiring it, is but a Prologue to a Farce or a Tragedy; or, perhaps both. Knowledge will forever govern ignorance: And a people who mean to be their own Governors, must arm themselves with the power which knowledge gives.[2]

A High School Curriculum for Leadership

Having realized the dependence of democracy upon education, yet noticing a lack of educational facilities and opportunities, led a distinguished American educator, Noah Webster, to note the discrepancy between theory and practice.

> This appears to me a most glaring solecism in government. The constitutions are *republican,* and the laws of education are *monarchical.* The *former* extend the civil rights to every honest and industrious man; the *latter* deprive a large portion of the citizens of a most valuable *heritage.*[3]

One of the first Americans desirous of translating into practice the ideal of equal educational opportunity was Thomas Jefferson. His *Bill for the More General Diffusion of Knowledge,* regarded as a landmark in the history of educational thought, stood in direct opposition to the Puritan concept of education for the élite, a chosen aristocracy. Jefferson's *Bill* called for a system of free education for every child in the elementary grades, affording the opportunity to the more talented students to go on to the secondary grades and college as well. The bill was defeated in the Virginia legislature in 1779. Jefferson was ahead of his times, but he implanted an ideal in the minds of many Americans; for subsequent educational history in the United States has been the unfolding of Jefferson's concept of equal educational opportunity for all.

Americans had to be convinced first of the necessity of elementary education. The nineteenth century saw the fulfillment of the ideal of universal elementary education. School societies composed of public-spirited citizens organized to influence state legislatures to make provisions for schools. Many leaders—Carter and Mann in Massachusetts, Barnard in Connecticut and Rhode Island, Stowe in Ohio, Wiley in North Carolina, and Mills in Indiana—arose to champion the cause of universal education. By means of writings and contacts with leaders of government these men helped inaugurate a free and universal system of free education. The rapidly growing economy of the nation, brought on by the Industrial Revolution and westward expansion, gave impetus to the role education was to play in removing the barriers between the privileged and propertied and the underprivileged and deprived.

As America entered the twentieth century, universal free elementary education was cherished as a democratic ideal. This ideal, however, had not yet been extended to the secondary level. The Latin grammar school, serving only the children of the privileged few, characterized colonial secondary education. Unable or unwilling to adopt a democratic outlook, the Latin grammar school—a transplanted European institution—gave way to a more American institution, the academy. Seeking to educate and to train young men, and later young women, not merely a privileged few, for a place in American democratic life, the academy won a place on the American educational scene at the beginning of the nineteenth century. The curriculum of the academy offered more than a classical course preparation for college studies. Influenced by scientific and technological progress, as well as business and industrial expansion, the academy's curriculum favored a more practical and utilitarian education.

Still the academy was not regarded as an extension of the elementary school in the educational ladder providing free schooling. The academy, maintained for the most part under private auspices, lacked the democracy characterizing the elementary school, where an education was obtained at public expense. Students financially unable to attend the academy terminated their formal education at the elementary level. To provide an extension of universal free education from the elementary to the secondary school level inclusive, the high school, a new institution in education, was established. The city of Boston opened the first American high school in 1821, an example followed by other cities. The Law of 1827 in Massachusetts, passed under the leadership of James G. Carter, required a tax-supported high school for every town having more than five hundred families. The need for the high school for the extension of equal educational opportunity was finally recognized. Approximately five hundred high schools could be recorded by 1870.

Opposition to the power of the state to tax for high-school education arose and climaxed in the famous Kalamazoo Case of 1874, which established a legal precedent for all states in permitting tax funds to be used for high-school education. The decision sought to establish an ideal whereby the state could "furnish a liberal education to the youth of the state in schools brought within the reach of all classes."[4] By 1890 the number of high schools increased to over 2,500, a fivefold increase in twenty years. More than 10,000 high schools with an enrollment nearing the million mark characterized American education in 1910. The extension of the ideal of equal educational opportunity to the secondary level can be seen better in the percentage of students attending high school. In 1900 an estimated ten per cent of all high-school age children were attending secondary schools. By 1950 as many as 85 per cent were enrolled in America's high schools.

As a high-school education became available to an increasing percentage of America's youth, attention was focused upon its curriculum. Still influenced by the European pattern, the American high school until the twentieth century was designed primarily for students intending to go to college. But not all high-school students aspired to a college education. This contradiction between the aim of the students and the curriculum of the high school had to be resolved.

In 1893 the National Education Association's Committee of Ten sought to clarify the contradiction by claiming that the American high school was established primarily to prepare for life rather than for college. Because the percentage of high-school graduates who went on to college was insignificant in comparison to those who terminated their education at the end of high school, the committee maintained that the high school's

> main function is to prepare for the duties of life that small proportion of all children in the country—a proportion small in number, but very important to the welfare of the nation—who show themselves able to profit by an education prolonged to the eighteenth year, and whose parents are able to support them while they remain so long at school.[5]

Although still requiring all students, whether college-bound or not, to pursue practically the same subjects, the report implanted the idea that secondary education, as well as elementary education, should be for all American youth.

With the report of the National Education Association's Committee on the Reorganization of Secondary Education in 1918, a revolution took place in secondary education, now no longer for the select few but for all youth up to the age of eighteen. Its report, "The Cardinal Principles of Secondary Education," presented new aims for the high school in its role of preparing youth for life: health, command of fundamental processes, worthy membership, vocational efficiency, civic competence, worthy use of leisure time, and ethical character.[6] The distinctive role of preparation for college gave way as the American high school admitted all students desirous of an education beyond the elementary school. The impact of the expanding role of the high school can well be seen in 1950, when approximately 85 per cent of youth of high school age was enrolled in high school, with only about 25 per cent of the graduates to attend college.

Believing to be in conformity with the principles of democracy, of equal educational opportunity for all, educators changed the character of our American high schools. Instead of being regarded as training ground for future intellectual leaders of our democracy, the high school changed to a comprehensive institution. The comprehensive high school was to have a student body composed of all youth, with distinctions among them reduced to insignificance. Non-academic subjects were introduced for those unable to pursue the academic subjects of mathematics, science, and foreign languages. No youth, despite his native intellectual ability, was to be deprived of a high-school education. If he could not adjust to the curriculum, then the curriculum should be adjusted to him. The educational philosophy of John Dewey was invoked to justify the watering-down process in the curriculum to meet the heterogeneity of the high-school population; for the child, according to Dewey, was to determine the quantity and the quality of learning.

Evaluating the quantitative effect of the growth of the American high school, one cannot but see the realization of the democratic ideal of equal educational opportunity. No other country has ever attempted to teach so many youth for so long a time. American youth can acquire just about as much learning as they wish. It would be futile to question the fact that our American democracy has not been benefited by an increasingly better educated electorate. The common good has undoubtedly been served. Education for the élite has given way to education for all. Steps for universal free college education have begun to be taken. Evaluating the qualitative effect of the American high school, however, raises profound questions.

CHAPTER TWO

The American High School Challenged

THE criticism of America's educational system since the successful launching of Russia's Sputnik has centered about the high school. Here, it has been pointed out, we are failing to provide a foundation for advanced work, notably for the sciences, but for other scholarly pursuits as well.

Statistics show the steady removal of academic subjects from the high-school curriculum to give place to life adjustment courses. Until recently half of our country's high schools did not even offer chemistry and physics. Only about 24 per cent of our students studied algebra, 11 per cent geometry, 4.3 per cent physics, and 2 per cent trigonometry.[1] A similar situation has existed in the study of foreign languages.

Sputnik, of course, has made a re-evaluation of the American high school more pressing and more immediate. But American educators have leveled serious criticism at the anti-intellectual content and spirit of the high-school curriculum before Sputnik was conceived. Robert M. Hutchins and Mortimer J. Adler objected to the inroads that progressive education practices, based on the pragmatism of John Dewey, had made in American education.[2] The romantic approach to the child's interests and felt needs lay largely at the basis of the anti-intellectualism characterizing our educational system. In a famous statement of Dewey, we find that

> Not knowledge or information, but self-realization, is the goal. Literally we must take our stand with the child, and our departure from him. It is he, and not the subject matter, which determines both quality and quantity of learning.[3]

Commenting on the above statement of Dewey, Mortimer Smith, writing as a lay critic of American education in 1949, evaluated such a philosophy of education and demonstrated the breakdown and chaos it produces in actual practice,

> for it teaches that there are no intellectual or moral standards of knowledge, that no subject is intrinsically of any more value than any other subject; in the end it reduces education to a vast bubbling confusion, in which training in mechanical skills is put on a par with the development of mind and imagination, in which hairdressing and embalming are just as important, if not a little more so, than history and philosophy.[4]

It is true that in the attempt to educate the masses the traditional academic curriculum seeking to train the mind had to give way to more vocationally oriented subjects. For as much as one-third of the total high-school population has been estimated as being non-verbal, or incapable of profiting from the mental discipline offered by the traditional academic subjects of mathematics, science, and foreign languages. In expanding its population, the American high school characterized by selectivity and homogeneity at the beginning of the twentieth century has been replaced by a heterogeneous high-school population composed of youths once channeled into various occupational trades at the age of sixteen. It is now felt that in extending equal educational opportunity for the many—a genuine democratic ideal in education—we geared our schools to mediocrity.

Scientists and businessmen, as well as educationists, have been pointing out the disastrous effects of the softness in American education. We have succeeded in attaining equal educational for all. We have failed in attaining another democratic ideal: the training of the gifted for leadership. Democracy in education has been misinterpreted. It is not the same type of education for all without discrimination but an opportunity to develop one's God-given talents to the best of one's abilities. The attempt to equalize all, applied to the field of economics, would be branded as socialistic.

Dr. Arnold O. Beckman, president of Beckman Instruments, Inc. and president of the Los Angeles Chamber of Commerce, has offered a businessman's view of the failure of a wrong interpretation of democracy in education. America's schools have not produced the steadily increasing need for more scientists and engineers. It is especially in the field of mathematics, a subject by its nature which trains for clear thinking, that incompetent teachers have not inspired our youth who remain unqualified for advanced training in college.[5]

Dr. James R. Killian, Jr., as president of the Massachusetts Institute of Technology and special assistant to President Eisenhower for science and technology, called for more emphasis "on the value of intellectual discipline and on the importance of content rather than method. In recent years we have been managing to get along in the United States by displaying an attitude of condescension toward hard work in our schools."[6]

The belief is widespread now that democracy in education should be interpreted as affording the ultimate in opportunity for the development of one's talents. Not only is a well-educated citizen vital to the perpetuation of democracy, but intellectual leaders to deal with the pressing problems of international tension and rivalry are necessary also. As a matter of fact, one of the more recent advantages of a liberal education that has been pointed out is that democracy needs trained minds, the very *raison d'être* of a liberal education. No longer are educators labeling as aristocratic the training of the gifted few for intellectual leadership and regarding a liberal education as a luxury for the privileged class; for a mind disciplined with a liberal education is free and equipped to lead in a democratic society, whose very foundations rest on the notion of the freedom of man's mind and will.

Hutchins has written forcefully of the changed conception of the role of a liberal education.

> Liberal education was the education of rulers. It was the education of those who had leisure. Democracy and industry, far from making liberal education irrelevant, make it indispensable and possible for all the people. Democracy makes every man a ruler, for the heart of democracy is universal suffrage. If liberal education is

the education that rulers ought to have, and this I say has never been denied, then every ruler, that is every citizen, should have a liberal education.[7]

Bestor has even been more poignant in noting the relationship between democracy and education. He claims that liberal education is a bulwark of freedom, that anti-intellectualism is a betrayal of democracy, and that the interpretation of democracy in education includes not only giving to the many the intellectual training once reserved for the few but also giving an advanced education for the ablest.[8]

Can the American high school offer a liberal education? Can it prepare intellectual and scientific leaders, America's gifted, to lead a great nation? What ought to be done in our American high schools to prepare, not merely quantitatively, but qualitatively, for democracy's future leaders?

The recent criticism of American education has created the spirit appropriate and even essential to make serious evaluations of the high-school curriculum. The pendulum has swung from mediocrity to excellence. In the words of the Rockefeller Report on Education, "The Pursuit of Excellence: Education and the Future of America,"

It is possible for us to cultivate the ideal of excellence while retaining the moral values of equality. Whether we shall succeed in doing so is perhaps the fundamental issue in the development of our human resources. A challenge must be recognized before it can be met. Our society will have passed an important milestone of maturity when those who are the most enthusiastic proponents of a democratic life are also the most vigorous proponents of excellence.[9]

What ought to characterize a high-school curriculum aimed at the pursuit of excellence? With a firm realization that schools exist to teach the mind to think and that the traditional subjects of mathematics, sciences, and foreign languages help train that mind to think, a curriculum for leadership must consider more than just an accumulation of subjects. Curriculum construction for leadership and the pursuit of excellence cannot be accomplished by addition and subtraction, a method common in curriculum revision. Rather, the basic aim and over-all objective in seeking to train leaders should be examined and established. This basic aim or over-all objective should then lead to a philosophy of a curriculum for leadership, with subjects arranged and fitted into a tight pattern.

CHAPTER THREE

The Philosophy of a Curriculum for Leadership

SINCE the first days of formal schooling the notion of the curriculum has been tied to the very purpose of education. To a large degree the curriculum is a philosophy of education in day-to-day classroom practice. When asked what he believed boys should be taught in school, Aegesilaus, king of Sparta, suggested that they learn what to do when they will become men. Regarded as having a functional origin the curriculum looks forward to preparing youth to take their place in life. Lack of a clear perspective in this regard would only result in a curriculum, or choice of activities in school, that would be without purpose and thus become unsystematic and disorganized. The dynamic notion of the curriculum as the sum-total of all the organized experiences, which the school plans for and provides, stipulates the need for guiding aims.

In seeking a philosophy of a curriculum for leadership the fundamental question is, "What should be the basic aim or over-all objective of the high-school curriculum?" Each student trained for leadership is to receive a general education, a common reservoir of knowledge basic to any type of specialized studies in the future. Since the goal of the proposed curriculum is aimed at producing Catholic leaders, the desired broad reservoir of knowledge must be unified by religion, both as a subject of study and more especially as the determinative principle of the whole educational process.

A knowledge of our common cultural heritage should make up this broad reservoir of knowledge no matter in what field the student may someday wish to devote himself. This is not to minimize the importance or even the necessity of specialization today. Specialization, on account of technological advance and growing research in every field, has become a desired necessity. Specialization, however, to the detriment of a common cultural background, leads to the development of a fish at home only in the waters of its own choice, without even an appreciation of unknown waters. Such a type of specialization leads to a stinted, stunted mind, which is lost outside its own field and cannot comprehend the broad horizons of human knowledge. Knowledge is like a circle, a united whole. One can segment for intensive study a part of that knowledge. But when the part is studied apart from the entire circle then the intimate relations between the parts of the circle are not perceived. Intellectual confusion and ignorance necessarily result.

A philosophy of a curriculum for leadership could find no better inspiration than from Cardinal Newman's *Idea of a University*. Stressing the interrelatedness of all knowledge, yet limiting its acquisition to but a relatively small portion of it by a single individual, Newman presents the basic qualities of a mind that is the product of a

off portion from portion, and operation from operation, except by a mental abstraction; and then again, as to its Creator, though He, of course, in His own Being is infinitely separate from it, and Theology has its departments towards which human knowledge has no relations, yet He has so implicated Himself with it, and taken it into His very bosom, by His presence in it, His providence over it, His impressions upon it, and His influences through it, that we cannot truly or fully contemplate it without in some aspects contemplating Him.[7]

As we would consider one superficial if he were to study Persian culture without first knowing something about the beliefs and institutions basic to an understanding of the Moslem world, so it would be superficial to attempt a common cultural background for future leaders of Catholic thought if in religion the principle of unity were ignored. Religion, as a subject of study in itself and as an integrating force upon all other subjects, serves as the unifying force in the common cultural background needed for leadership. In constructing the high-school curriculum for leadership, religion provides the general themes covering the four years of study, to which the other subjects in the curriculum are subordinated and depend upon for complete and more meaningful development and exposition.

Trained to think with a broad reservoir of knowledge as a background, unified by religion, one attains the over-all objective of the Catholic high-school curriculum for leadership.

The mere statement of the over-all objective, however, does not suffice. The curriculum must be so patterned and organized that the student, the future leader of thought, will obtain a broad reservoir of knowledge as his intellectual foundation for future study and even specialization.

Three criteria should determine the pattern and organization of a curriculum for leadership: continuity, sequence, and integration. Continuity refers to the connection between the different subjects studied from year to year. Sequence concerns itself with the connection of materials offered within each subject. Both continuity and sequence find their necessity in the mind's way of learning: preceding from the known to the unknown, from the simple to the difficult, from the concrete to the abstract, from the near to the remote. Traditional curricula have amply fulfilled the two criteria of continuity and sequence. In so far as the criteria of integration is concerned, however, traditional curricula have not been too successful. Integration seeks the connection of subjects with each other in the same year and with the entire pattern and organization of the curriculum.

A number of attempts based on information derived from studies in the psychology of the learning process have sought to provide integration in the curriculum. In an analysis of some of these attempts there unfolds a synthesis of the best elements in each.

Applying Herbart's doctrine of apperception which states that the student learns new material in terms of the old and that learning becomes more meaningful and interesting when associations can be formed in the mind, teachers of different subjects sought to plan cooperatively, especially for time placement. Designated a correlated curriculum, examples like the following would be incorporated into the curriculum: American history and American literature would be taught during the same academic year for a particular class of students, with the works of literature studied in the English class at the time that the particular historical period was being considered in the history class. Thus, students could see a more meaningful relationship between the two academic disciplines. Similar efforts at correlation of subjects have been made with history and geography, mathematics and science.

The influence of Hegel's philosophy of history on curriculum development lay in the formulation of the culture-epoch approach. Herbart and his follower Tuiskon Ziller emphasized that man's mind could best acquire knowledge if it pursued the development of that knowledge throughout the history of mankind. Accordingly, distinct historical periods should divide the curriculum, with all aspects of culture characteristic of the period studied, as politics, military events, art, music, and literature: i.e., how man lived and thought in a given period. Thus would Hegel's idealism, whereby history became the means employed by the Absolute to unfold itself in the affairs of mankind, be put into practice in the field of curriculum development.

Another attempt to make the curriculum more meaningful was the broad fields curriculum. Here a fusion or grouping together under one heading is made of closely related school subjects. Rather than teach history, geography, government, economics, sociology, as separate and distinct subjects, all are brought together and taught in one course—the social studies. Similarly, physics, chemistry, geology, and astronomy would be fused into a course in the physical sciences. Botany, zoology, physiology, and hygiene would be classified under the life sciences. General mathematics would replace the individual subjects of arithmetic, algebra, geometry, and trigonometry, and emphasis would be placed on presenting to the students the basic mathematical skills and understandings from each field. Art, music, and literature, both from the original English and translations of great writings from other languages would appropriately be taught in a course entitled the humanities.

One of the more common approaches to putting meaning into the curriculum has been the core curriculum plan. Basically a merger of two or more subjects, the core curriculum requires a period of time longer than the usual time allotted to subjects forming a "core," the most common of which is English and the social studies. One teacher is placed in charge of the core program, and since he is with the same class for a longer time this teacher also serves as the guidance counselor. Broad units of work rather than the traditional subject-matter divisions characterize the learning experiences of the core program. The vast majority of core programs are found at the junior high-school level. There is more of a difficulty in obtaining qualified teachers on higher levels for the core curriculum.

The proposed curriculum for leadership is based on an analysis and synthesis of the above approaches, keeping also in mind the three criteria required for a meaningful curriculum pattern and organization.

The Philosophy of a Curriculum for Leadership

Each of the four years of the high-school program would have a broad general theme around which the specific subject matters would revolve and would in each case contribute to an understanding and fuller exposition. The four broad general themes, in turn, would seek to attain the over-all objective of the curriculum for leadership: a common reservoir of knowledge. The two subjects of religion and history, in particular, contribute to the formulation of the four broad general themes, both for logical and psychological organization and presentation. Thus, the four-year high-school course* would be divided as follows:

Freshman Year

1. The World that God Has Created
   Religion—God as the Creator of the Physical World
   Science—Survey of Physical Sciences
   Mathematics—The Science of Numbers as a Means of Communication
   English—The Science of Language as Means of Communication
   Art—A Means of Human Expression
   Music—A Means of Human Expression
   Moral Guidance—God the Lawgiver

2. Ancient and Medieval Life and Culture
   History—Ancient and Medieval History
   Literature—Ancient and Medieval Literature in Translation

---

* Included in this outline are only the courses that contribute directly to the exposition of the general themes in each year.

A High School Curriculum for Leadership

Sophomore Year

1. Man in the World that God Has Created
   Religion—Man's Nature and Means for Happiness
   Science—Survey of the Biological Sciences
   Moral Guidance—Commandments of God and the
   Church

2. Modern Life and Culture up to the 20th Century
   History—Modern World History up to the 20th
   Century
   Literature—Modern World Literature up to the
   20th Century

Junior Year

1. Knowledge and Love of Our Country
   Religion—The Good Citizen in American Life and
   Society
   Moral Guidance—Select Moral Social Problems

2. American Life and Culture up to the 20th Century
   History—American History up to the 20th Century
   Literature—American Literature up to the 20th
   Century

Senior Year

1. Adjustment to the World in which We Live
   Religion—Rational Basis of Our Religion
   Moral Guidance—Select Moral Problems brought
   on by Modern Living

2. Twentieth Century Life and Culture
   History—Main Events of the 20th Century
   Literature—20th Century World Literature

The philosophy of a curriculum for leadership, then, will stress the interrelatedness of all knowledge. In such a manner only can the student obtain that desired broad reservoir of knowledge which he can use as a background for further specialization in a fragment of knowledge. Studies in the psychology of learning support attempts at viewing knowledge as a unity. A curriculum with broad general themes facilitates one's transfer of training into desirable directions. According to Judd's theory of generalization, a high-school curriculum organized with the interrelatedness of knowledge in mind would conform to the nature of the learning process since

> no experience remains in the human mind in isolated form. One never thinks of an item which is presented to one's senses without relating it to the other experiences which make up the contents of one's thinking. If the relations in which ideas are brought together in one's mind are purely accidental, as they are when a train of ideas passes through the mind in periods of idle fancy, then the individual gains little for his present training or future adaptation. If, on the other hand, the relations established by attentive thinking are carefully guarded and critically perfected, it is possible in a most productive way for action and for later constructive thinking.[8]

The laws of memory discourage the study of detached units, separate facts, unrelated items. Transfer of training is minimized, for logical connection has not been achieved and material learned becomes more and more meaningless with time. It is no wonder, then, that the memory has so often been referred to as the "faculty of forgetting." In the humorous vein of students' reasoning as to the futility of study, "The more we study, the more we know; the more we know, the more we forget; the more we forget, the less we know. Therefore, what's the use of study." A meaningful curriculum, one organized according to broad general themes and in which each subject contributes to a fuller and richer understanding of the themes, establishes logical associations between learned material. Logical memory implies understanding, the seeing of relationships between the whole and parts, and parts from parts as well. "The pupil who remembers well ideas which are logically related is the pupil who is attentive, who grasps the significance of schoolwork, who organizes his work."[9]

The placement of subjects in the proposed curriculum for leadership is taken up in the next chapter and it is hoped that the words of Judd can apply to it:

> Such a curriculum will make a single piece of information carry to the student not only a bare kernel of truth, but a whole network of suggestions by which the central truth connects with the rest of the world.[10]

CHAPTER FOUR

A Proposed Curriculum
for Leadership

FUTURE leaders of a democracy must be trained. Fundamental to any specialized training is a general education. In a curriculum for leadership the attainment of the over-all objective, a broad reservoir of knowledge, comprises the idea of general education, which the NEA Educational Policies Commission has designated as "common learnings," or those "learning experiences which *everyone* needs to have, regardless of what occupation he may expect to follow or where he may happen to live."[1]

Providing a common cultural background to future leaders obviates one of the most serious consequences of specialization: isolation of leaders of thought from one another. Lacking a common ground they cannot communicate with each other. Yet scientists, diplomats, educators, and all leaders in a democracy do share a common objective. Each leader views this objective in the light of his specialty. But an absorption in one's specialty to the extent of being unable to comprehend its role in the promoting of the common good can lead to a chaotic separatism among democracy's leaders.

A curriculum for leadership, then, must include in its pattern and organization a group of subjects, in addition to the four broad general themes, which all students would pursue. Opportunity for electives, moreover, is still possible. Courses comprising the curriculum for leadership are now discussed. Each student pursues the subjects contributing to the exposition of the general themes, thus insuring a broad reservoir of knowledge, and then is permitted to pursue a more specialized program depending on his future professional interests and academic career.

I. *The Subjects of Study*

The subject of religion plays an important role in any Catholic curriculum. The proposed curriculum for leadership would, in addition to the integrating function of religion, divide its study into religious doctrine, or truths to be believed, and moral guidance, or truths to be lived. Although the distinction between dogma (*regula credendorum*) and moral (*regula agendorum*) is made, the exposition of the principles of moral conduct should be presented with the firm realization that no system of moral can exist without a system of set beliefs or dogma. A standard of conduct needs dogmas, for what one believes should determine how one acts.

The study of Religious Doctrine would be divided as follows:

Freshman Year: The World that God Has Created. The study of God as the creator of the physical universe is the object of this course and is correlated with the science course surveying the physical sciences. The student is led to an appreciation of what God has done for man to live in this world. This course could very well be modeled on Part I of *My Way of Life* by Fathers Farrell and Healy, which is entitled "God and His Creatures."[2] Two hours a week would be assigned to this course.

Sophomore Year: Man's Role in the World that God Has Created. Based on Part II of *My Way of Life*, "Man: The Image of God," this year's religion course would deal with the nature of man, what means God has afforded a weakened but redeemed nature to achieve happiness, as Grace, the Sacraments, and the virtues. Three hours a week would be devoted to this course in religion, which is correlated with the course in science surveying man's biological nature.

Junior Year: Knowledge and Love of Our Country. The role of the good Catholic in American life and society would comprise this year's religion course as the student pursues a study of American history and literature. Emphasis on the social virtues guiding man's family, political, and economic relations would be the main objects of consideration. Two excellent works are suggested for preparing this course: *Christian Social Principles*[3] and *You Can Change the World*,[4] a Christopher handbook, also to be considered in group and in individual vocational guidance.

Senior Year: Adjustment to the World in which We Live. The science of apologetics should be offered the student, whereby he may be able to defend adequately his religious beliefs and practices. The course should be so presented that it will leave the student convinced on a rational basis in conformity to his present intellectual development of the need and value of religion so that his life and thinking would serve as a defense and explanation of his religious faith. Both the Junior and Senior Religion courses will take up three class periods a week.

The program in *Moral Guidance,* a class period weekly for the four years, would be divided as follows:

Freshman Year: God as the Lawgiver for All Creatures. As a moral being man's conformity to the moral law is considered, with an appreciation of the order that is meant to exist in the world, if it is governed by law as God has intended.

Sophomore Year: The Commandments of God and the Church. These commandments would be so presented as to convince the student of the manner in which God and His Church seek to have him live by the moral law.

Junior and Senior Years: Select Moral Problems. Students should be afforded the opportunity of having discussed frankly the problems of moral behavior confronting them. By means of students' questions the course would be geared to the needs and interests of the students. A priest would be the ideal teacher for such a course. Opportunities for individual moral guidance should be made possible by having priests available for this purpose in all Catholic high schools.

Most schools assign five class periods a week to the study of religion. The above program in assigning less does not intend to minimize the importance and role of religion in the curriculum. This role is not necessarily minimized by eliminating a class or two. "Religious truth," as Newman viewed it, "is not a portion but a condition of general knowledge."[5] As religion contributes to the formulation of the four broad general themes each subject in the curriculum is developed in relation to the "condition" of general knowledge. Where subject matter would be repeated in a religion course and in other courses, then that subject matter is included in the so-called "secular" study. Thus, a history of the Jewish people in the old Testament, the life of Christ, and the history of the Church are treated in history courses, where the full impact of these factors in history can be evaluated. Taking them out of the historical context is a needless separation of knowledge. Moreover, the idea that religion is the center and core of the Catholic curriculum is enhanced by such an arrangement.

History and the Social Studies

History is the study of man's past under the aspect of change and continuity in the various modes of human living, as political, social, economic, intellectual, and religious. This concept of history includes man's development in the areas of the social sciences. Thus considered, the student is afforded the opportunity to analyze and to appreciate the changes and improvements in the different areas of man's life. Political life is not viewed apart from man's economic struggles or his religious aspirations throughout the periods of history. Specialization in the social sciences of sociology, economics, or political science becomes more appropriate in college. High school can provide the basis and over-all general historical background for specialization in a particular area of man's development.

Few high schools today attempt to present a panoramic view of man's past in all of its historical periods. Ancient history has for the most part been dropped completely from high-school programs. Medieval history has been receiving but a cursory glance. Or ancient and medieval history have been treated in world history courses attempting to cover in one year the entire history of mankind. In such general courses, ancient and medieval history have been regarded as only introductory matter. Yet no one can deny the importance of tracing man's development in all areas from its earliest records. The historical approach can serve as an introduction to all fields of knowledge. Man's failure in one generation can turn out to become but the necessary step to success in a succeeding generation. This attempt at a panoramic view of man's past can provide a fund of knowledge. Many facts will have to be eliminated. But obtaining the panoramic view of the broad outlines of history is far superior. The details can be fitted into the outline in later study and specialization. A panoramic view is far more lasting than the accumulation of isolated facts.

The history and social studies program will then be divided as follows:

Freshman Year (5 hours weekly): How man has progressed in the world God has created through the ancient and medieval periods.

A Proposed Curriculum for Leadership

Sophomore Year (5 hours weekly): A study of world history from the beginnings of modern times up to the twentieth century.

Junior Year (5 hours weekly): A study of the history of the United States up to the twentieth century.

Senior Year (2 hours weekly): A study of twentieth century history, the position of leadership enjoyed by the United States and the challenge to the free world by totalitarian philosophies, with a comparison of the divergent economic and political systems of democracy and totalitarianism. The stress placed on developments in the twentieth century in various nations leads to a better appreciation and understanding of the different peoples making up the world. Their ideals and aspirations can be seen further in the literature course running concomitantly with the history course. Thus is promoted the idea of neighbors in one world.

Literature

The literature courses would include selections from great writings in all languages, showing how the ideas of the writers exemplify the life and thought of the people of the periods. Few question the value of the classics as these works enable the reader to delve into the thinking of great minds. Yet how many American students ever get the opportunity to read them in school? Since language is a barrier, translations of the great writers should be made available. Selections from the writers of ancient and medieval times should be offered for, at least, a perusal by the student. It is true that in this proposed curriculum English literature is sacrificed. But do not the great writers of other peoples, as Dante, Camoëns, Schiller, Montaigne, Calderon, deserve at least a passing glance from American students? Ought not some excerpts from Vergil, Horace, Plato, Homer, and other literary masters of ancient Rome and Greece be made available as well? Efforts at making it possible for American students to read non-English works in translation have already been made. Select modern writers of continental Europe occupy a section in *English and Continental Literature* by Brewton, Lemon, Sharp, and Abney. Although primarily a text for college students, *Our Heritage of World Literature* by Thompson and Gassner could be revised and adapted for high-school students;[7] for the selections have been so selected and arranged that it can be seen how these works of literature "have entered into the very bloodstream of our culture."[8] Thus we have the advantage of correlating the study of the subjects of history and literature.

Maintaining religion as the integrating subject *par excellence,* such works and authors as the Psalms, the Eucharistic poems of St. Thomas Aquinas, selections from the Fathers of the Church, should be considered. An elective course in the senior year could be made available to students desirous of delving further into the field of English literature.

English Grammar and Composition

No one can be a leader until he first masters his native language. A thorough grasp of the elements of grammar and the mechanics of the English language of necessity claim an important role in the making of the future leader. Both written and oral expression must be perfected as quickly as possible.

The value of a scientific study of the English language as is done in grammar and composition can be seen in an English teacher's definition of "good English."

> Good English is that medium of communication by which man uses his faculty of speech to express the good, the true, the beautiful. It is the language by which he relates the thoughts, the feelings, the desires and conflicts of his inner life. It is the gift God has given man to distinguish him from the strict category of the animal world. It lives and changes as man lives and changes. It is a tool of exchange, flexible and adaptable, yet conforming to the standards set down by society for whose purpose the language exists.[9]

In itself, then, the study of the English language commands an important place in the training of the future leader—he who must use language, both written and oral, to influence the minds of others. Language bridges the gap between minds. It communicates thoughts, feelings, attitudes, ideals. Or what Aristotle, the father of logic, would refer to as the primordial identity of speech with reason. Thought and language are one and inseparable. Clarity and preciseness of language reflect clarity and preciseness of thought. In high-school English grammar and composition classes students can obtain the indispensable tool of exactness of expression to be further strengthened in the college courses of logic and philsophy.

As a means of expression language affects every other discipline in the curriculum. Skills acquired in reading and writing to communicate ideas in other subject matters necessarily help or hinder one's total academic success. So tied with success in other studies is verbal skill that many liberal arts colleges use as a predictor of general academic success the "Verbal Aptitudes Test" of the College Entrance Examination Board.

A recent survey conducted among approximately five hundred educators, businessmen, government officials, librarians, law-school deans, editors, and publishers found many of them calling English "the most important subject in the curriculum,"[10] for a command of the English language is needed by leaders in all fields. The emphasis on the study of language in the curriculum for leadership may help overcome the charge that "the great bane of science and social studies is mechanical repetition of incomprehensible words and phrases."[11]

As every Catholic teacher is a teacher of religion because of the central position of religion in the curriculum, every teacher is a teacher of English, because English is the language common to the studying of the other academic disciplines in the curriculum. All teachers, therefore, should share the responsibility of improving the communicative talents of their students. Although the rules for writing and speaking may be devised and taught by the English teachers, they are to be enforced by all teachers in oral and written recitations and assignments. Furthermore, the different disciplines can strengthen the important role of language in the curriculum. Science teachers can point out the rigidity of precise technical language more so than the literature teachers who deal with fluid language, changing its meaning in different contexts. Religion and social studies teachers can impart the importance of the clarification of terms before entering discussions. The foreign language teachers can call attention to the close relationship between words in different languages and at the same time caution on minor shades of difference. Mathematics, art, and music teachers can show how the ols used in their subjects are expressions of thought—a point stressed in the freshman year of the curriculum for leadership in demonstrating the different forms of human expression that God has made possible.

Since style can be improved by analyzing the writings of great authors, a selected number of different types of literature should be chosen, not primarily for content, but for development of style. Where the literature classes stress the life and thought of a given period, English composition classes would study an essay, a novel, a poem, a drama for demonstrating how various types of writing communicate ideas. It is suggested that this aspect of the study of language be carried on throughout the four-year program according to the needs, interests, and progressive development of the students.

As to the five class periods assigned to English, three ought to be spent exclusively for the study of grammar in the freshman year, two in the sophomore and junior years, and one in the senior year, allotting the remaining classes each year to the study of literature.

Science

A general over-all view of the natural sciences should be presented. The freshman year would deal with the physical sciences: chemistry, physics, geology, astronomy, while the sophomore year with the life sciences: biology, zoology, psychology, with more of an emphasis on man's physiological and psychological make-up. Some may classify the study of these natural sciences as only a "smattering." Yet a knowledge of the basic elements of each of these natural sciences would give the student a far better, rounded-out knowledge than the studying of either one or two of them as is more commonly done now.

For students contemplating scientific careers, courses in physics, chemistry, and biology on a more advanced level would be offered in the junior and senior years. For future majors in engineering, mechanical drawing could be made available. These courses have been arranged in the science program offered in the curriculum for leadership. A program is thus provided in the high-school years to give students a mathematical and scientific background to help them in college studies. It is the lack of this background that has caused many a college student in the natural sciences and mathematics to fail or to transfer his program through inability to pursue college work.

Yet the science courses have a purpose besides that of training future scientists. All cannot be scientists, but all leaders need to know the value and place of science in the modern world. Although no one questions that science and technology hold the key to military superiority, as well as economic and industrial expansion—aims of great concern in the present "cold war"—the status of education and research in science and engineering in this country during the last decade has been described as being "in a continuous cycle of enthusiasm and apathy."[12] The teaching of science and mathematics in our schools has been deplored both for content of the courses and lack of adequately prepared teachers.

As "the health of our society and our ability and capacity to assume increasing responsibilities as a world power depend heavily on the quality of scientific education throughout the country,"[13] educational and political leaders must appreciate the commanding role of science in determining the destiny of the civilized world.

Pope Pius XII made note of the unity between religion and science as the "idea of God finds confirmation in every new development and progress of scientific knowledge."[14] Figures, formulae, and discoveries—this language of science—Pius XII saw as also expressing the harmony in the work of the Creator as seen in His creation.

Catholic leaders of thought in all fields should appreciate the connection between science and religion and how mankind can be aided by the progress of science in the different areas of man's life. Scientific progress has and always will support the *philosophia perennis,* upon which Catholic thinking is so largely dependent. "It is only by means of mutual understanding and cooperation that there can arise a great edifice of human knowledge that will be in harmony with the higher light of divine wisdom."[15] This can be the especial contribution of the Catholic to the role of science in present-day thinking.

Since a curriculum for leadership seeks to train the mind with qualities of intellectual leadership, the distinctive values of science courses in this area should not be disregarded. As human learning starts with sense knowledge, science courses make use of man's sense equipment to become aware of the objective world which exists independently of the mind. A creative outlook and an inventive spirit receive encouragement. In dealing with objective reality, loyalty to facts is fostered and the importance of objectivity is taught. With a curriculum characterized by religious unity the student sees science as revealing God's handiwork, the good that can come out of material things, and how man can subdue the forces of nature and utilize matter for the betterment of mankind.[16]

The survey courses in the physical and biological sciences taken by all students and correlated with the religion courses in the freshman and sophomore years and the science program in the proposed curriculum for leadership exemplify the emphasis and approach needed in scientific education today.

Mathematics

Viewed at first as the language of numbers and symbols, the basic elements of each branch of this science should be considered. Sacrificing content in the early years for vitalizing the subject would in the long run

Modern Foreign Languages

The study of modern foreign languages is to be determined by the needs and interests of the students. Future specialists in the natural sciences, mathematics, and engineering could well begin a study of German in high school. Many technical scientific writings have been written in German or published in full or abstracted form in German even if translated in other languages. Russian should be the language studied by the future leader in government or diplomacy. A Romance language, preferably French because of its necessity as a reading requirement for graduate degrees, should be considered for non-science majors.

Yet it would be a mistake to look upon the study of the modern foreign languages simply as tools. As Jacques Barzun so poignantly put it, "a tool is a dead, unchanging thing; a language lives."[18] To understand fully the thought, the customs, the literature of a foreign people one must know their language. Recent methods of teaching the modern foreign languages by grouping the processes of reading, writing, speaking, and thinking into a single fluency have contributed to making foreign tongues "living" languages for the American student. With a scientific exposition of the rules of grammar as a basis, the newer approaches to language study could well have the student speaking a foreign tongue in three years of high-school study. Thus would leadership be promoted for producing future members of the diplomatic corps who would not be handicapped by lack of the facility of expression in a foreign post. Furthermore, they could penetrate the very thoughts, aspirations, and ideals of foreign peoples as they would possess the means of communicating thought and feeling in their own language.

If, as has already been the case in some educational systems, the study of modern foreign languages is begun in the higher elementary school grades, then the modern foreign language can hold an even more prominent place in the curriculum for leadership. With the basic grammar having been studied, more time can be devoted to literature. Thus, the study of French literature, for example, can be integrated with the courses in history and English literature. Students would then read in the original foreign language the literary works of the historical period covered in the curriculum for that year.

Art and Music

These two fine arts should be studied as forms of expression given to man by God. A half-period—actually a full period given every other week in the freshman year in the theory and appreciation of art and music—would help provide a well-rounded personality. Further, great works of art and music should be made available to the student in each respective historical period. Teachers of languages could indicate how the same ideas expressed in writing have been also expressed in the works of art and music. Teachers of history would place emphasis on these works as expressions and reflections of the ideals and aspirations of the people at their time in history. The ideal, of course, would be to establish a course combining the subjects of history, literature, art,

and music into a course entitled the Life and Culture of
a given period. However, the lack of teachers competent
in all such areas of the culture of a given historical period
deems such a course impractical, although desirable.

Vocational Guidance

An hour a week of group guidance conducted every
year, supplemented by individual conferences, with the
discussion of such topics as different types of careers,
vocational planning, college entrance requirements, schol-
arships, would comprise the vocational guidance program.
Father Keller's *Careers That Change the World*[19] is rec-
ommended as a *sine qua non* for all students to read and to
discuss in class for it suggests opportunities whereby students can become leaders in various fields of influence.

Physical Education

The maxim *mens sana in corpore sano* is accepted and
advocated for the full development of the individual.
Physical stamina is necessary for the future leader. However, athletics must be subordinated to studies. This ought
not prevent a well-coordinated athletic program from
being conducted *after* classes. No one questions the les-
sons of fair play and teamwork that are acquired from
active participation in sports.

II. *The Programs of Study*

Three suggested programs in the curriculum for leadership have been delineated: classical, modern humanities, and science. The availability of competent teachers, needs and interests of the students, laboratory facilities may necessitate modifications. The specifics must always stand secondary to the philosophy of this curriculum which seeks primarily a meaningful and challenging curriculum providing a broad reservoir of knowledge as a basis for leadership.

Classical Program

Based on the humanistic ideal of the Renaissance, the distinctive feature of this program is the study of Latin for four years. Students aspiring to the priesthood would find a twofold advantage in pursuing this program. Latin for them is regarded as a necessary tool for their philosophical and theological studies. A universal Church has kept a universal language as a means of communication and liturgical worship. The humanist ideal of mental discipline would benefit all students, whether or not Latin will ever be used as a tool. For students desirous of specializing in the study of languages the value of Latin cannot be overestimated. All the Romance languages are derived from Latin. The study of the development of the English language will necessarily involve a study of its indebtedness to Latin. The study of Greek would be desirable in a classical program. Few high

TABLE 1

CLASSICAL PROGRAM
(Subjects with class periods per week)

Freshman		Sophomore		Junior		Senior	
Religion	2	Religion	3	Religion	3	Religion	3
English	5	English	5	English	5	English	3
History	5	History	5	History	5	History	2
Latin	5	Latin	5	Latin	5	Latin	5
Physical Sciences	5	Biological Sciences	5	Mathematics	5	Mathematics	5
Mathematics	5	French or Russian	5	French or Russian	5	French or Russian	5
Moral Guidance	1	Moral Guidance	1	Moral Guidance	1	Moral Guidance	1
Vocational Guidance	1	Vocational Guidance	1	Vocational Guidance	1	Vocational Guidance	1
Art	½					Elective	5
Music	½						

schools remain in this country that offer Greek, and its study, outside of college majors in the Classics, is pursued by candidates for the priesthood in the first two years of their college program in the minor seminary.

A choice of either of two foreign languages is offered, depending on the student's interests and future occupational needs. Since French is a language requirement for graduate degrees, a student can well take the opportunity to fulfill a requirement which can later turn out to be burdensome in the midst of a research program. The need for more Americans to know Russian has become obvious with the rising political power of Russia in the world.

The elective in the senior year of the classical program can be a science course or English literature.

Modern Humanities Program

The study of modern foreign languages differentiates this program from the other two programs in the curriculum for leadership. Designed primarily for future diplomats and professions in the fields of politics and economics, the study of modern foreign languages, in conjunction with the history courses, affords the student the knowledge of the basic tools required for international communication and understanding of international political and economic problems.

The elective in the senior year can be a science course or English literature. A discussion course in current political and economic problems could be suggested for a select group of interested students.

Conclusion

SUCH is the proposed curriculum for leadership. As is the case for all innovations, new problems arise. Two fundamental problems emanating from the adoption of this proposed curriculum are teachers and textbooks. Especially in the fields of history and literature, present teachers may not have the required knowledge for teaching the works of ancient and medieval literature and non-English works. Present history teachers may require more reading in the ancient and medieval periods.

At present difficulties also exist as to textbooks, especially because of the general themes characterizing the four years of high-school study. No course, however, should be synonymous with a text. Until texts are written specifically for such a curriculum, it rests with the teachers to supplement present texts with explanations of the general themes and mimeographing of materials not yet available in textbooks. Although these problems can be considered disadvantageous in adopting this proposed curriculum, it is felt that the advantage of producing leaders by a more meaningful curriculum is fulfilling a more pressing need.

High schools with small enrollments would find it difficult to adopt this curriculum. Their percentage of students capable and desirous of pursuing such a curriculum would be so small that it would not be to the best practical interests of arranging the teachers' schedules of courses. Large high schools can set aside at least a classical and a scientific group in each high-school year for pursuing this suggested curriculum for leadership.

It is suggested that minor seminaries adopt this curriculum for their high-school programs. Students for the priesthood are a select group of better-than-average students intellectually and, furthermore, are trained to acquire a taste for serious study. Their environment in the seminary, moreover, supplies them with desirable study habits. A curriculum for leadership in a seminary fulfills the high ideal afforded to learning in the priesthood set forth by Pope Pius XI.

> Indeed, in all ages the Catholic clergy has distinguished itself in every field of human knowledge; in fact, in certain centuries it so took the lead in the field of learning that the word "cleric" became synonymous with "learned."[1]

Truly, the priest should be trained for intellectual leadership.

This suggested curriculum for leadership has never been put into practice. It merely offers a philosophy for a curriculum, with suggestions to fill in the outline drawn from this philosophy. Modifications would necessarily result in the adoption of this curriculum as circumstances of the particular situation warrant. However, as for all suggested plans for curriculum revision and improvement, experience is the crucible in which they are refined and perfected.

Notes

NOTES FOR INTRODUCTION

1. H. G. Rickover, *Education and Freedom* (New York: Dutton & Co., 1958).

2. P. H. Witty, "Today's Schools Can Do Much for the Gifted Child," *The Nation's Schools,* LVII (1956), No. 2, p. 72.

3. Pope Pius XI, *The Catholic Priesthood* (Washington: NCWC, 1936), pp. 41-43.

4. J. L. Spalding, *Means and Ends in Education* (Chicago: A. C. McClurg and Co., 1897), p. 220.

5. J. T. Ellis, *American Catholics and the Intellectual Life* (Chicago: The Heritage Foundation, Inc., 1956), p. 16.

6. In the Prefatory Note to Monsignor Ellis' book, *op. cit.,* p. 10.

NOTES FOR CHAPTER ONE

1. *The Works of Daniel Webster* (Boston: Little, Brown & Co., 1885), Vol. I, p. 403.

2. Madison to W. T. Barry, Aug. 4, 1822, G. Hunt (ed.), *The Writings of James Madison Comprising his Public Papers and Private Correspondence, including numerous Letters and Documents now for the First Time Printed* (New York: Putnam, 1910), Vol. IX, p. 103.

3. Quoted from A. O. Hansen, *Liberalism and American Education in the Eighteenth Century* (New York: The Macmillan Co., 1926), p. 235.

4. Stuart v. School District No. 1 of Kalamazoo (1874), 30 Mich. 69, 75.

5. National Education Association, National Council of Education, "Report of the Committee of Ten on Secondary School Studies" (1893), p. 51.

6. National Education Association, "Report of the Commission on the Reorganization of Secondary Education," *U.S. Bureau of Education, Bulletin 35* (1918).

NOTES FOR CHAPTER TWO

1. *U.S. News & World Report* (Oct. 7, 1955).

2. R. M. Hutchins, "The Philosophy of Education," in R. N. Montgomery (ed), *William Rainey Harper Memorial Conference* (Chicago: University of Chicago Press, 1938), pp. 35-50; M. J. Adler, "In Defense of the Philosophy of Education," in National Society for the Study of Education, 41st Yearbook, *Philosophies of Education*, Pt. I, Chap. 5, (Bloomington, Ill.: Public School Publishing Co., 1942).

3. Cited by Ernest Cobb in *One Foot on the Ground* (New York: G. P. Putnam's Sons, 1932), p. 21.

4. M. Smith, *And Madly Teach* (Chicago: Henry Regnery, 1949), p. 24.

5. A. O. Beckman, "A Businessman's View on the Failure of Education"; *U.S. News & World Report* (Nov. 30, 1956), p. 84.

6. J. R. Killian, Jr., "White House Missile Expert Takes a Look at U.S. Schools," *U.S. News & World Report* (January 24, 1958), pp. 83-85.

7. R. M. Hutchins, *The Conflict in Education in a Democratic Society* (New York: Harper & Brothers, 1953), p. 84.

8. A. Bestor, *The Restoration of Learning* (New York: Alfred A. Knopf, 1955).

9. *The Pursuit of Excellence: Education and the Future of America* (New York: Doubleday & Co., 1958), p. 17.

Notes

NOTES FOR CHAPTER THREE

1. J. H. Newman, *The Idea of a University* (New York: The America Press, 1951), p. 68.

2. *Ibid.,* p. 153.

3. *Ibid.,* p. 193.

4. C. Dawson, *Enquiries into Religion and Culture* (London: Sheed and Ward, 1933), p. 115.

5. C. Dawson, *Understanding Europe* (New York: Sheed and Ward, 1952), pp. 242, 243.

6. Newman, *Idea of a University,* p. 44.

7. *Ibid.,* pp. 67-68.

8. C. H. Judd, *The Psychology of High School Subjects* (Boston: Ginn and Co., 1915), p. 414.

9. W. A. Kelly, *Educational Psychology* (Milwaukee: The Bruce Publishing Co., 1952), pp. 94-95.

10. C. H. Judd, "The Relation of Special Training to General Intelligence," *Educational Review,* XXXVI (1908), p. 39.

NOTES FOR CHAPTER FOUR

1. Educational Policies Commission, *Education for All American Youth: A Further Look* (Washington: National Education Association, 1952), p. 241.

2. W. Farrell and M. J. Healy, *My Way of Life* (Brooklyn: Confraternity of the Precious Blood, 1952).

3. Sister M. Consilia O'Brien, O.P., *Christian Social Principles* (New York: P. J. Kenedy & Sons, 1941).

4. J. Keller, *You Can Change the World* (New York: Longmans, Green and Co., 1948).

5. Newman, *Idea of a University,* p. 84.

6. J. E. Brewton, B. Lemon, R. A. Sharp, L. Abney, *English and Continental Literature* (New York: Laidlaw Brothers, Inc., 1950).

7. S. Thompson and J. Gassner, *Our Heritage of World Literature* (New York: Dryden Press, 1956).

8. *Ibid.*, p. v.

9. Sister M. Harriet, O.S.F., "Defense of Good English," *The Catholic Educator*, XXX (1960), p. 340.

10. J. Mersand, "English Meets the Challenge," *The English Journal*, XLIX (1960), pp. 62-63.

11. *General Education in a Free Society* (Cambridge, Mass.: Harvard University Press, 1945), p. 116.

12. H. C. Kelly, "National Program for Education in the Sciences," *School Review*, LXVII (1959), p. 396.

13. *Ibid.*, p. 401.

14. Pope Pius XII, "Modern Science and the Existence of God," in V. A. Yzermans, *Pope Pius XII and Catholic Education* (St. Meinrad, Ind.: Grail Publications, 1957), p. 56.

15. Pope Pius XII, "The Perennial Philosophy and Modern Science," in Yzermans, *op. cit.*, p. 154.

16. C. F. Donovan, "Educational Values of Science Courses," *The Catholic Educational Review*, LV (1957), pp. 89-95.

17. A. E. Meder, Jr., *Modern Mathematics and its Place in the Secondary School*. Reprinted from the October, 1957, issue of *The Mathematics Teacher* by the Commission on Mathematics of the College Entrance Examination Board, p. 13.

18. J. Barzun, *Teacher in America* (Boston: Little, Brown & Co., 1945), p. 136.

19. J. Keller, *Careers That Change the World*. Garden City, N.Y.: Permabooks, 1950.

NOTES FOR CONCLUSION

1. Pope Pius XI, *The Catholic Priesthood* (Washington: NCWC, 1936), p. 41.

Index

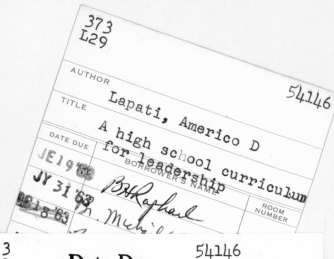